HEARTFELT

...A DEEP EMOTION

HARSH PARMAR

Copyright © Harsh Parmar
All Rights Reserved.

This book has been published with all efforts taken to make the material error-free after the consent of the author. However, the author and the publisher do not assume and hereby disclaim any liability to any party for any loss, damage, or disruption caused by errors or omissions, whether such errors or omissions result from negligence, accident, or any other cause.

While every effort has been made to avoid any mistake or omission, this publication is being sold on the condition and understanding that neither the author nor the publishers or printers would be liable in any manner to any person by reason of any mistake or omission in this publication or for any action taken or omitted to be taken or advice rendered or accepted on the basis of this work. For any defect in printing or binding the publishers will be liable only to replace the defective copy by another copy of this work then available.

Contents

Acknowledgements

Hi!

Thank you to all my readers who gave some of their precious time to read this book.

This book is not an effort of one person alone. First of all, I would like to thank my parents who gave their support and encouraged me for writing.

Then I would like to offer my thanks to my friends for their invaluable support and time that they have given for the completion of this book.

I am also thankful to the entire team of Notion Press that gave me the opportunity to publish my work so that it can reach to millions of readers around the globe.

Last but not least, I once again thank my readers who chose my book over the others and found some time out of their schedule to read this book.

To those who love with whole of their heart...

1. FOREVER LOVE

Attached together insanely
Fell in love madly,
No worry what will happen next
If we were together, I'll handle the rest.
Like a pearl in the ocean
Your eyes shine brightly,
No wonder that
I love you so deeply.
Walking on the beach,
To the point no one can reach;
Holding hands of each other,
Spend our lives together.
Wetting down in the rain,
Wishing all hopes to sustain;
Kissing on the street,
Without worrying about moral discreet.
Happy moments we cherish,
Sad ones we perish.
Being by your side in your happiness,
Gives satisfaction and fulfillness.
Kissing on forehead when you cry,
I look up at the sky;

HEARTFELT

Looking at the stars in the eve,
I wish you never leave.
May our love last forever,
We never fall apart ever.

2. LOVE AROUND US

Sun shines brightly in the sky,
I look into your eyes.
World around me spins,
Snow falls in the winter chills.
Your golden hair,
Flaunts in the air.
Your glossy lips,
I want to kiss.
Your pearly eyes glisten,
Like sea shines in the sun.
When I look at you,
There is always something new.
Our love is unconditional,
Memories we have made are special.
Pictures of our, are hanging on the walls,
The fun we had in the snowfall.
Walk in the garden,
Will never be forgotten.
Atmosphere is filled with love,
Stars in the evening shine above.
Pleasant flowers all around,
Romantic song plays in the background.

HEARTFELT

Mild breeze blows,
Ground is spread with flowers of rose.
Hold my hand and never let go,
If you leave, my life will be full of sorrow.
Our moments together will make memories,
This relationship plays sweet melodies.
Destiny is on our side,
My future with you is bright.
We will be together,
I will adore you forever.

3. LOVE IS IN THE AIR

Love is in the air,
Life is so fair.
By the seaside,
With you beside.
On the top of mountain,
Under the fountain.
Shower in the rain,
Blood rushing though the vein.
Fluttering bushes,
The wind wooshes.
Beautiful flowers,
Nature is full of colors.
Stars shining,
The moon rising.
The warmth in your arm,
I cannot get away from your charm.
Citylights at night,
Dims the moonlight.
Reflection of lights in the water,
Makes it appear like gold and silver.
Feeling you with arms curled,
I hope we stay forever coupled.

In your breath, in your smell,
I feel something special.
Your silliness,
Gives me happiness.
How you tease,
I want the moment to freeze.
Atmosphere around us,
Sings in chorus.
How adorable we look together,
Our love will be remembered forever.

4. TRUE LOVE NEVER DIES

True love never dies,
Memories bring tears in the eyes;
It wants you by my side,
Whether we are in city or countryside.
True love never dies,
My heart screams and cries;
It wants to make memories,
That will be remembered for centuries.
True love never dies,
It can handle all the lows and highs;
It can withstand every blow,
You just need to calm down and go slow.
True love never dies,
With every hug and fight, it multiplies;
Being with each other gives serenity,
True love lasts for eternity.

5. FORBIDDEN LOVE

Two souls
Wanting each other,
To stay
Together forever.
Dance to the ball
Sing with the koel,
Ride with swan
Make every moment special.
Take care
Of one another,
By one another's side
Always and forever.
They had wish to enjoy
Starry nights in one another's arm,
And travel around the world
Rest where there is calm.
Lying on green grass
Staring up at the sky,
They both thought
They would never say goodbye.
They met each other
Hiding from people's eye,

If people find out
They both would die.
Unfortunately, people found out
Their love was forbidden,
They had to separate
Had to forget their affection.
Both cried at night
Their pillows got wet,
Tears rolled down their eyes
They had nothing but to regret.

6. HEARTBROKEN

You are leaving now
But my feelings don't fade away,
My love is so deep…
That watching you leave, my eyes weep.
Moon and stars remind me
Of our night long talks,
Life has lost colors…
But I keep staring at your pictures.
The day starts
Thinking about you,
Pictures are the only memories I am left with…
Your love over my loneliness was a sheath.
I am heartbroken now
With scars in the heart,
Giving an everlasting pain…
That has let my happiness drain.
I beg forgiveness for the sins
And the mistakes that I made,
Now I can do nothing but mourn…
Because the damage has been done.
My silent tears
Speak a thousand words,

When I cry under my pillow…
For my pain and sorrow.
The promises, the trust,
The love, the feelings, the night long talks,
Everything now seems fake…
And I am suffering this heartbreak.

7. LOST LOVE

If we were together
Things would have been nice,
With you beside
I would talk to you with my eyes.
We would walk along the empty road
With your hands in mine,
I will wake up everyday
By seeing your face in the morning sunlight shine.
When you would cry
I would wipe your tear,
If we were together
You would have nothing to fear.
We would enjoy together the long nights,
Away from the city and the lights.
We would admire the beauty of nature,
That will give us moments to capture.
We would enjoy movies together,
With arms around each other would be so better.
We would hug each other every time,
Whether its morning or bedtime.
We would walk on the sand by the sea,
And watch the gulls when they flee.

A peck on cheek would make my day,
Wind would carry your wishes to me when you are away.
At times I felt weak
You were by my side,
Since you were there
I didn't have to make my feelings hide.
Sometimes I did make you hurt,
Then I wanted it to revert.
But now our love is lost,
Just like sunlight melts the frost.
The promises that were meant to be kept,
Now mean nothing and I try to forget.
Every part of me hates myself,
For letting you go as I couldn't do anything else.
My heart weeps all the time,
Because you are no more mine.
People say it hurts,
The pain of it feels the worst.
Standing below the night sky
Watching the fireflies fly,
I wish I could turn my emotions off,
So, I can no longer feel grief and loss.

8. COME BACK NOW

We are no more together
Perhaps we were never meant to be for each other,
Come back now
I want to be with you forever.
I don't know without you
I will live how,
You are my life
Come back now.
Come back now
I miss you everyday,
You act like
Your feelings are on a holiday.
Come back now
I feel empty,
World appears colorless
And the pain feels heavy.
My mind bursts
With the flood of memories,
Come back now
And restore the harmonies.
Come back now
Nights are no more calm,

And days no more shiny
Thoughts have turned to storm.
Come back now
Life has become hell,
Misery is a friend
And eyes have become tear filled well.
Nights scream to me
And days call out loud,
Come back now
Cries with me every passing cloud.
Not for me
But for vow,
Without you, I cannot live
Come back now.

9. SOME FEELINGS NEVER CHANGE

Some feelings never change,
Whether you love or hate me
They will remain the same.
Sometimes they drive you off the shore,
In your thoughts;
But you are whom I always seek for.
Cuddling in our cozy little bed,
Sitting with you with your head on my chest
The world seemed full of roses red.
Your head resting on my lap,
Gives you all the comfort
Sometimes you even took a nap.
Crying for each other at night,
Wetting the pillow
Forgetting every tear when we got each other's sight.
The promises that we made,
Are now broken;
But the feelings don't fade.
A part of me says to forget,
Because everything has ended

But heart says hold on to days that were your life's best.
I still pray,
We will cross each other's path
Some day.
Doesn't matter if it's strange,
Waking up everyday with your memories;
Because some feelings never change.
Some feelings never change.

10. I AM LOST

I am lost
In the air,
With the clouds.
With the sand grains
I fly,
To the far ends.
With the river
Flowing down the hill,
I travel down the slope.
Sunrise and sunset
Passes like time,
I stay unnoticed and I am not fine.
Leaves has shed
Trees are barren,
Life was once like heaven.
World around me screams
Head bursts with thoughts,
I am not me and I am lost.
Rain reminds me of you
Tears roll down my eyes,
Everything happened was a lie.
Nights are not calm

Nightmares have become permanent,
I am not happy with our detachment.

• 19 •

9 7 9 8 8 8 6 2 9 7 1 2 6